Honi the Circlemaker

D1520305

Honi the Circlemaker

Eco-Fables from Ancient Israel

Barry L. Schwartz

Illustrated by
Stewart J. Thomas

Friendship Press • New York

To Nadav, Talia, Noam
and all children

Editorial Offices:
475 Riverside Drive, New York, NY 10115
Distribution Offices:
P.O. Box 37844, Cincinnati, OH 45222-0844

Manufactured in the United States of America
Printed on recycled paper

Library of Congress Cataloging-in-Publication Data

Schwartz, Barry L.
    Honi the circlemaker : a journey in ancient Israel / Barry L.
Schwartz.
      p. cm.
    Summary: Retells the wondrous deeds of Honi-the-
Circlemaker, who wandered over the land of ancient Israel
planting carob seeds and spreading goodwill.
    ISBN 0-377-00251-8
    1. Honi, ha-Me' aggel, 1st cent. B.C.—Juvenile literature.
2. Talmud—Biography—Juvenile literature. 3. Legends, Jewish.
[1. Honi, ha-Me' aggel, 1st cent. B.C. 2. Jews—Biography.
3. Folklore, Jewish.] I. Title.
BM530.H66S39   1993
[B]   92-33715
                                           CIP
                                           AC

Contents

Preface

To the Reader Who Is a Storyteller

Stories are meant to be shared. I hope that after you read these stories you will become a storyteller. The tales of Honi the Circlemaker lend themselves to being read aloud on many different occasions. Honi's journey through the land of Israel encompasses the four seasons. Recounting his adventures might enhance celebration of the holidays that mark each turning of the year:

"The Dream" is a story of spring, appropriate for Passover and Easter.

"A Blessing" and "Two Palms" are stories of summer, appropriate for Shavuot and Pentecost.

"The Rainmaking" is a story of autumn (when rain begins to fall in the land of Israel), appropriate for Sukkot.

"These and These" and "The End of the Circle" are stories of autumn—winter, appropriate for Channukah and Christmas.

All the stories celebrate the flora and fauna of the land of Israel, especially the trees. Consider reading them at the Jewish New Year of the Trees (Tu Bishvat) and the festivals of Israel (Lag B'omer and Yom HaAtzmaut). Likewise, these tales might add to observance of civic festivals like Arbor Day and Earth Day.

Stories are also meant to be embellished. You might like to retell them in drama form. Think about assigning parts, adding props and costumes, pantomime, and even music. I am sure that Honi would be pleased!

Stories help explain the way we view our world. We tell stories, first and foremost, for the sheer joy of listening and marveling and finding ourselves intrigued. But stories can also be powerful learning tools. The storyteller is also a teacher. The tales of Honi the Circlemaker can deepen our appreciation of ancient Israel in a number of ways:

Geography

Honi the Circlemaker indeed encircles the whole land of Israel in the journey from his home in the Galilee, along the Jordan river to Jericho, past Jerusalem and inland, around the Dead Sea into the Negev desert, through B'ersheva and back north. It's hard to believe that Israel is virtually a dot on the map, a little country only a few hundred miles long and a fraction of that distance wide. Yet in this little land are a snow-covered peak in the north and a great desert in the south. Along the coast of the Great Sea, as the ancient Israelites called the Mediterranean, are flat, sandy beaches. Just a day's journey inland, in the Judean foothills and Jerusalem, the terrain turns rocky and rugged.

Honi the Circlemaker was from a small village in the Galilee, in the north of Israel. In the spring, the

Galilee's rolling hills are covered with grass and delicate wildflowers. Barley and wheat sprout in the valleys, olive orchards and vineyards cling to the steeper ground. Here and there are groves of white and pink blossoming almond trees and the occasional fig or carob tree. Ah, yes, the carob tree. Have you ever tasted a raw carob? Carobs look like giant brown pea pods, and the shell is brittle and dry. But it is the shell, not the seeds, that is eaten. Keep chewing and as the texture softens many people compare the taste to bittersweet chocolate.

History

The history of ancient Israel during the life of Honi is full of drama and political intrigue. The turbulent period of the first century B.C.E. is of continuing interest to both Jews and Christians, because it sets the political and religious stage for the emergence of rabbinic Judaism and early Christianity. The decrepit Hasmonean dynasty, supposed heirs to the Maccabees, is on the verge of collapse. The two brothers vying for the throne in the story "These and These" are Hyrcanus II and Aristobulus, who engaged in a civil war spanning the years 67–63 B.C.E. By then Rome had stepped into the political power vacuum left by the internal strife and already controlled large parts of the country. It is thus possible for Honi to have encountered Roman soldiers near Tiberius, as he does in the story "A Blessing." The Roman commander, Pompey, captured Jerusalem after a three-month siege in 63 B.C.E. It marked the beginning of an era of increasing repression and despair, which culminated in the destruction of the Second Temple in 70 C.E.

Ethics

I consider these stories a series of eco-fables. They are all very much concerned with our relationship to the land and evince the rabbinic ethic called in Hebrew *kavod habriyot*, reverence for creation. Reverence is born of wonder, what Abraham Joshua Heschel called "radical amazement" at the existence of the world. So many of us walk sightless among miracles. Honi seems to be graced by a special awareness of the miraculous. And he understands that reverence leads to responsibility. Out of gratitude for the blessings of the earth that sustain us, Honi dedicates his life to fulfilling a pledge that "just as my ancestors planted for me, so I will plant for my children."

The Circlemaker embodies other virtues esteemed by our tradition. Outstanding among them is *rachmanut*, compassion. Honi proves himself ready to come to the aid of people he knows ("The Rainmaking") and people he does not know ("Two Palms"). At the same time, Honi demonstrates a passion for *din*, justice. Honi is steadfast in his refusal to bow to tyranny ("These and These"). According to our ancient Talmudic sages, justice and compassion are the two qualities that sustain the world.

It is worth noting that on two important occasions compassion, on the part of others, saves Honi's life. Honi's townfolk join hands to support him ("The Rainmaking"), as do complete strangers (the Nabateans in "These and These"). In the final episode ("The End of the Circle"), it is out of love that Honi's community pledges to complete his unfinished circle.

About the Man Who Is Called "The Circlemaker"

Honi Ha-Me'aggel, which is the Hebrew original of Honi the Circlemaker, was the real-life name (actually nickname) of a remarkable man who is thought to have lived in the land of Israel just over two thousand years ago. What we know of Honi comes to us from the Talmud, a massive commentary on the Hebrew Bible containing a mixture of laws and stories. The Talmud is also ancient; the first part was compiled about 200 C.E. and the latter part was completed by 500 C.E.

Honi is mentioned in a tractate of the Talmud called *Ta'anit*, which relates many legends about miracle workers. Though Honi is a memorable figure, still there are almost no biographical details about him. In fact, there are really only three brief stories about Honi in the Talmud. The first involves a time when Honi is said to have brought rain to his drought-stricken land by drawing a circle and standing within it while beseeching God. An embellished version of that tale becomes "The Rainmaking" in this collection. A second story tells of Honi's encounter with a man planting a carob tree and his subsequent sleep of seventy years (whereupon Honi awakes and nobody believes he is still alive). This tale is the basis for my stories "The Carob Tree" and "The End of the Circle." A third story (recounted by Josephus) amounts to an alternative account of Honi's demise at the hands of soldiers loyal to Hyrcanus II. This tale is incorporated into the latter part of my story "These and These."

As for the other stories, they are wholly the product of my imagination. But you should know that bits and pieces of every story have been inspired by sources I have encountered. For instance, the blessing of the tree in "A Blessing" is from an ancient midrash. So too is the account in "Two Palms" of a tree bearing fruit after being grafted to another. And the words of Honi to the almond tree in "The Dream" are attributed to the Greek writer Nikos Kazantzakis.

Though so little is said about Honi in the Talmud, he is a beloved figure among school children in Israel. Say the name Honi the Circlemaker and you will hear about carob trees, rainmaking, and falling asleep for a long time. In the course of the tale about the rain, the Talmud hints darkly that Honi's free thinking and independent ways ran him afoul of the religious authorities of the day. Likewise, recall that a competing legend claims that Honi did not die peacefully in his sleep, but was caught up in a political scenario. Undoubtedly the man who was Honi was more complex than the one in our memory and fiction. Yet Honi's love of his land and his people touches us across the span of two thousand years. Come and join his circle!

Honi the Circlemaker

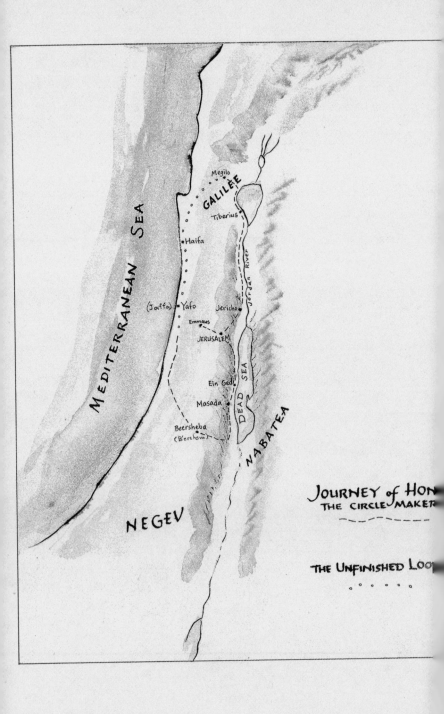

MEDITERRANEAN SEA

Megilo

GALILEE

Tiberius

Haifa

Jordan River

(Jaffa) Yafo

Jericho

Emmaus

JERUSALEM

DEAD SEA

Ein Gedi

Masada

NABATEA

Beersheba
(B'ercheva)

NEGEV

JOURNEY of HON
THE CIRCLE MAKER

- - - - -

THE UNFINISHED LOO

o o o o o

1

The Carob Tree

Once when Honi the Circlemaker was quite young and was still called by the plain old name Honi, he was out walking and saw an old man planting a carob tree.

Honi asked the man: "How long will it take for this tree to bear fruit?"

The man replied: "It will take seventy years."

Honi asked him: "Why are you planting that tree? Are you sure you will live another seventy years?"

The man replied: "Just as my ancestors planted for me, so I will plant for my children."

2

How Honi the Circlemaker Got His Name

Now, just how did Honi get his nickname, the Circlemaker?

Some people said it was because of the way he looked.

Some people said it was because of the way he worked.

And some said it was because of the way he talked.

The way he looked

Honi was a mountain of a man. His ample belly was rotund. So were his bulging biceps. But it was Honi's head that was most round. Despite a big bushy beard, Honi was as bald as could be. Above his brows, he was barren as the moon—which is why everybody remarked that Honi's head was so perfectly shaped.

The way he worked

Honi was a barrel maker. He made big barrels as tall as a man, and little barrels as small as a baby. But big or small, Honi's barrels were perfectly round at each end. Anybody inspecting his work, from the top or the bottom, was sure to see two identical circles.

The way he talked

Honi was a jovial man, with a ready smile and a gleam in his eyes. He was also learned in the Torah. Many people, even Rabbis, consulted Honi on points of Jewish law. Honi would patiently listen to a question, then nod his head and smile and begin. Well, according to this authority . . . but of course another authority has it that . . . and as you know, it says in Scripture that . . . Honi quoted so much Torah that—well, it could run you in circles and drive you mad!

3

The Rainmaking

One dry day, when the entire land of Israel was
suffering from a terrible drought, the people of Honi's
town gathered in his shop. "Help us," they pleaded,
"our water supply is gone; our prayers for rain remain unanswered."

"Do something, Honi the Circlemaker!"

This time Honi did not smile, for he knew how
serious the situation really was. Putting aside his
barrels, Honi strode out of his shop and into the town
square. As the townfolk gathered around in amazement, Honi drew a perfect circle with himself at the
center. Then looking skyward Honi said in a booming
voice: "Master of the Universe, your people beseech
me; now I beseech you. I shall not budge from this
circle until the sky has clouded and rain has fallen.
The sun by day, the moon by night, shall be witness.
Neither left nor right, forward nor backward shall I
move, until my people have been saved."

No sooner had he spoken, when the sky grew dark.
A tremendous thunderclap sent people scurrying for
shelter. The town square was quickly deserted, save
for Honi in his circle. Night came, pitch black and
filled with the sound of the howling wind. Peeking out
of their shuttered windows, the people saw nothing,
except when a flash of lightning illuminated Honi in
his circle.

At the break of dawn the winds died, but the sun
remained hidden in a blanket of gray. Then it started

to rain. A mere pitter-patter at first, which quickly turned into a driving downpour. In the midst of it stood Honi, motionless as a statue, streams of water cascading down his face into his beard. It poured and poured. The river overflowed its banks. The town was in danger of flooding. The town elders dashed from their homes to Honi.

"Do something, Honi the Circlemaker, or we shall all drown!"

Once again Honi raised his voice to Heaven. "Not for rains of destruction have we asked," exclaimed Honi, "but for rains of sustenance, rain that will fill our cisterns and quench our parched fields." At once the downpour slackened and the flood waters receded. A steady but mild rain continued to fall until the reservoirs were brimming and the ground was saturated.

But when the rains should have stopped, they did not. More slowly than before, but just as ominously, the waters started to rise.

As they had earlier, a group of elders scrambled over to plead with Honi. The Circlemaker had not moved from his circle. But he no longer stood erect, the elements having taken their toll on his vigil. His great head bowed, knees sagging, Honi looked in danger of collapse. As word spread of Honi's condition, people left their homes and gathered round as they had in the beginning.

"Be strong, Honi the Circlemaker. Stand up straight. Help us, as you have before."

It was still raining, but the people hardly noticed. Honi could barely hear all the voices urging him on, but when he managed to look up, he saw all the townfolk joining hands around him in a giant circle.

21

With a final burst of strength, he cried aloud: "Master of the Universe, let this rain bring blessing and not curse, sustenance and not deprivation, life and not death."

The people answered, "Amen."

And the sun began to shine.

4

The Dream (or How Honi Began His Quest)

One fine day in the land of Israel, Honi the Circlemaker closed the doors of his little shop while the sun was still high in the sky. Naturally, the village folk were curious.

"Where are you going, Honi the Circlemaker?"

"Such a fine day as this," replied Honi, "is meant to give praise unto the Creator."

With that, Honi headed for the hills. He smiled at the children, who called out his name. He nodded to the men and women. He strode out of the market place, past neat rows of houses with open courtyards and through fields of barley ripe for the picking and through fields of wheat growing taller.

Soon Honi was beyond the fields, climbing through groves of ancient, gnarled olive trees. In a few places there were also young almond trees. Their delicate pink and white flowers had blossomed in the month of Sh'vat and now lay scattered on the ground. In one corner a lone carob tree stood guard over everyone.

It was early in the month of Nisan. Spring had barely arrived, but the day was unseasonably warm. Honi was not yet accustomed to the heat. Little beads of sweat formed on his brow. Honi only sighed and smiled.

"Ah, the wonders of spring," he exclaimed, when he caught sight of purple irises poking out through

rocky soil. Honi searched for the brilliant red poppies that were another herald of spring, but they had yet to announce themselves.

Honi climbed steadily, and the land grew sparse and unyielding. Up here only shepherds roamed, their flocks of goats and sheep marking countless trails into the shrub-dotted hillsides. In his youth Honi had heard stories about the thick forests surrounding his village, which had been home to bears and even lions. In those days shepherds needed to be strong and brave, like the young King David.

Now the forests were gone, save for a single swath that clung to a wadi, a ravine, in the mountains. This wadi was Honi's destination. Honi found the ravine, and plunged into the tangle of green, following a narrow footpath that paralleled a small spring. The spring played hide-and-seek with Honi, waters gurgling above ground only to disappear and surface further along.

Honi came to a rock ledge high above the spring, shaded by pines, with a splendid view of the wadi

24

tumbling below. Removing his hat, he eased himself down and stretched out his legs. The soft breeze and quiet gurgling of the spring gently lulled Honi to sleep. As he was drifting off, a bird, calling from high in the treetops, momentarily stirred Honi awake. Its tune was vaguely familiar. Honi looked, but could not spot the bird. His eyelids again grew heavy, and Honi dozed. It is then that he had a dream.

High in the hills of the Galilee, on a lonely wind-swept hill, a young shepherd named Honi is looking for a patch of grass for his hungry sheep. Not so much as a shrub can be found. All is quiet, save for the whistling wind and an occasional bleat.

Honi searches and searches, but the land is barren. Honi too is hungry, but of course there is no fruit to be picked. Then Honi's sheep begin surging forward to a little valley between the hills. But they come to an abrupt halt and start milling about in confusion. Before them is a pasture, but the grass is not green. Almond and apple trees abound, but there is no fruit, nor even leaves. Birds perch on the branches, their beaks twittering, but not a sound is heard.

The sheep look to their shepherd. Honi looks at his sheep.

Honi is at a loss. What was this place? What should he do?

Honi sat down and thought, and he thought about the holy Torah, and a verse from the Torah lodged in his mind. Honi stood up and spoke to his sheep: "In the Book of Job is it not written: Siach la'aretz v'torecha, Speak to the earth, and it will teach you?" The sheep nodded in agreement.

Honi turned to the almond tree and said: "Sister, speak to me of God." And the almond tree blossomed.

25

Honi turned to the grass and said: "Brothers, speak to me of God." And the grass grew green.

Honi turned to the birds and said: "Friends, speak to me of God." And the birds sang psalms of praise.

Honi and his flock rejoiced and joined in the chorus of song. The Circlemaker began dancing about. . . .

A fly on Honi's nose stirred him awake. Honi shook his head and stroked his beard. "What a dream," he muttered.

The sun was well past its zenith; he ought to be heading home. On the way down, Honi thought about his dream.

Honi came again to the ancient olive grove, with the lone carob tree standing guard. Honi stopped to collect some of the long, brown carob pods, which have within them many seeds. Holding them in his hand he glanced up at the barren hills, remembering how once he had come upon a man planting carobs and remembering his dream.

And it was at that time and in that place that Honi the Circlemaker vowed to walk the land of Israel, and plant carobs wherever he went.

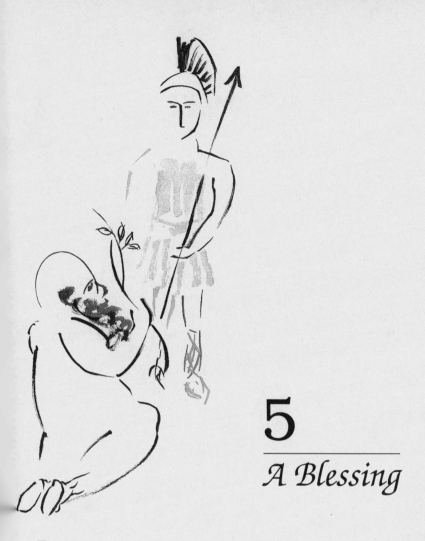

5

A Blessing

In the month of Sivan, soon after the Festival of the Firstfruits, Honi the Circlemaker began his walk across the land of Israel. Honi carried just three possessions: a walking stick, a flask of water, and a knapsack full of carob seeds. Naturally, the village folk were curious.

"Where are you going Honi the Circlemaker?"
"What is in your knapsack?"

"How long will you be gone?"

Honi only smiled. Everybody knew quite well what he had in mind. By now even the children had heard about Honi's dream and Honi's vow. They didn't believe he would do it, but here was the Circlemaker waving good-bye.

Honi came from a little village in the Galilee called Megilo. Some people say that is how he came to be called, in Hebrew, Honi Ha-Me'aggel, the Circlemaker. Megilo and M'agel sound so much alike. But as we have learned, there are many other reasons why Honi might have become known as the Circlemaker.

Honi was ready for the journey that would take him the length and breadth of the land of Israel. In truth he did not know how long he would be gone, only that he had a great task before him. From the heights of the Golan to the flats of the Negev, from the banks of the Jordan to the shore of the Great Sea, north and south, east and west, Honi would walk the land and plant his seeds.

Not more than two Sabbaths had passed when Honi's journey almost came to an abrupt end. Honi was on the road to Tiberius, having just finished planting and watering one of his seeds, when an officer of the Roman legion happened by.

"And what may be your business?" asked the curious officer, for it was rather odd to see a man bent over by the roadside, staring at something in the ground.

"Planting a carob tree, your honor," replied Honi.

"And do you have permission?" queried the officer, winking and smirking at the soldiers in his company.

"Why, no," replied a surprised and puzzled Honi.

"Then as punishment you must remain where you

are until I return from Tiberius. If you try to escape, you shall pay with your life."

With that the officer galloped off, leaving Honi in a cloud of dust on a very lonely and barren stretch of road under the hot Sivan sun, with barely a day's water supply in his flask.

Honi passed an uneasy night, but as the sun rose higher into morning sky he grew desperate. Honi surveyed the countryside and spied a solitary hill with a patch of green not too far off. Reasoning that he could still watch the road for the returning officer and hoping that the hill might reveal comforting shade and life-sustaining water, Honi hiked over to investigate. Honi began to feel parched and faint. He was at the point of collapse when to his delight Honi spotted a beautiful fig tree and by it a shallow pool fed by a subterranean spring.

Honi tarried in that lovely spot for two days. He ate of the tree's fruit and recuperated. Early on the third day, as he was surveying the horizon, he saw in the distance the approaching banners of the Roman legion. Loath to leave his little oasis, Honi nevertheless knew he must depart at once. Turning to bid the tree a final farewell, Honi said:

> "Tree, O Tree,
> with what shall I bless you?
> Shall I say to you:
> May your fruits be sweet?
> They are sweet already.
> Shall I say to you:
> May your shade be pleasant?
> It is already pleasant.
> That a stream of water should flow beneath you?

A stream already flows beneath you.
Therefore I say:
May it be God's will
that all shoots taken from you
be like you."

When the Roman officer rode up on his horse, he was astonished to see the Circlemaker in the exact spot he had left him.

"Tell me man," he commanded, "just how did you survive in this spot for three days?"

Honi recounted what had transpired, and when he was done the officer said: "Lead me to that very spot."

When they came to the pool, Honi looked around in

utter amazement. Not one, but seven fig trees, each identical to the other, encircled the shallow pool.

"Do you dare lie to me?" bellowed the officer. "You spoke of one tree only. What else haven't you told me?"

"By my life have I told you all, and all the truth," insisted Honi. "Only one thing have I neglected to recount." Then Honi repeated the words of the blessing he had uttered to the tree.

The officer stared at Honi, looked at the trees, and looked back at Honi.

"Go in peace," he said, and with a flick of the reins galloped off.

The Circlemaker looked on at the ring of trees, softly swaying in the afternoon breeze.

6

Two Palms

From Tiberius, Honi the Circlemaker hugged the shores of the Sea of Galilee until he came to the spot where the lake ended and the water flowed into the Jordan River. Here the Circlemaker paused to plant a whole grove of carobs before beginning his long trek down the river. Under the scorching sun of Av, Honi needed to stay close to the river, which at times looked like nothing more than a minor stream. Most of the flowers had gone to seed, and thistles abounded. Along the banks of the Jordan, tamarisk, willow, and poplar were plentiful, their creepers forming dense thickets that harbored many small animals, and a few big ones. Honi would climb to elevated spots above the river to plant his own trees.

Honi reached the ancient and so lovely city of Jericho at moonrise. The moon was completely full and at this early hour retained a pale orange glow low over the horizon. Honi always marveled at these spectacular summer moonrises and knew that this evening must be the fifteenth of Av. How fortunate he felt, for Honi also knew that in a few hours the young maidens of Jericho would be dancing in their white dresses. The fifteenth of Av marked the beginning of the vintage. Clusters of grapes lay heavy on the vines. To celebrate this harvest, the maidens would all borrow white dresses, not wearing their own so none would feel ashamed. Looking their best, they would

descend to the vineyards and dance and dance. Ah, they were beautiful. . . .

As the full moon of Av rose higher into the night sky it too changed into white garb for the celebration. Honi joined all the folk gathered to watch the dancing. The flutes struck up the joyful melodies, the maidens weaved in and out, the people clapped in rhythm. Honi too let himself be carried away by the festivity, so much so that he didn't feel the tug on his shoulder, until it was repeated a third and fourth time.

"Are you the Circlemaker?" whispered a soft voice.

Honi turned to see a young man, lean and tall, with imploring eyes. "Please help me."

The young man proceeded to spill out his heart to Honi. How he had fallen in love with a young maiden from another village, the village of Emmaus, a day's journey beyond Jerusalem. How her father would not hear of their union. How this maiden was the love of his life and he could not live without her.

"Do something, Honi the Circlemaker!"

Honi began talking further with the young man. There were questions in his mind about the young man's story, and, after all, the man had been a total stranger to him only minutes ago. But as they talked, Honi looked intently at the youthful face and began seeing himself, long ago. And Honi began thinking of a lost love. . . ah, but that was indeed so long ago, and. . . .

Honi did it. Yes, for the sake of that earnest, heart-sick youth, Honi did not continue south to the Dead Sea but turned inland and later that week reached Emmaus. He found the father of the maiden, an important official of the town, standing under a beautiful palm tree near the village square, conferring with his advisors.

"This palm tree will bear no fruit," the man was explaining. "We have grafted it again and again, and still it bears no fruit. The time has come to cut it down." The other men were nodding in agreement, when Honi stepped forward.

"This palm tree sees another palm tree in Jericho and longs for him with all her heart."

The men turned to see who had spoken. "Aren't you the Circlemaker?" exclaimed the father of the maiden. Honi then spoke at length with the father, who returned to his advisors with an order to send for a branch from the Jericho palm.

So they brought a branch from that palm in Jericho and grafted it on the one in Emmaus, and it immediately bore fruit.

Not long after these things, the official of Emmaus held a wedding for his daughter. The Circlemaker was not present, but if he had been, he would have seen delicious dates at the banquet table.

7

These and These

From Emmaus, Honi resumed his journey to the
south of the land of Israel. He planted many carobs in
the foothills of Jerusalem, tarrying there as the end of
Elul and the dry season drew near. In early Tishrei,
Honi made his way down to the Dead Sea, the lowest
point of elevation in the entire world. The land around
the stagnant, salty lake looked like baked clay in an
oven. Here Honi planted few carobs, doubting they
would survive. He marvelled, however, at the hardy
acacia trees, which stubbornly thrived in the parched
soil.

Honi's first destination was the oasis of Ein Gedi.
Refreshing pools of spring-fed water greeted him, as

did nimble gazelles that came down from the cliffs to drink with him. Honi collected dates from the palms that ringed the Ein Gedi settlement and, refreshed, set out for the trek past the desert fortress of Masada. The imposing rock, thrusting out from the sloping hills around, stood like a sentry at a border. Indeed, from this point on, Honi was travelling the fringes of the Judean kingdom, and the land was wild and dangerous. Honi sought only a glimpse of the Negev desert before turning north and back to the heartland.

Somewhere in the wilderness of Judea the Circlemaker began losing his way. The Judean desert was no place to be lost. Honi's water supply was already low. To travel in the heat of the day with so little water would be foolhardy. So Honi, finding no trees at all, left the path and climbed alongside the cliffs that bordered the route. Soon he found what he was looking for—a dank but cool cave, tucked in a crevice of the cliff, but with a narrow line of sight stretching for quite some distance.

Was it a mirage, or did Honi spot a shimmering band of movement on the horizon later that afternoon? The Circlemaker left the cave and moved closer to inspect. He beheld a caravan of Nabatean traders making their way to the markets of B'ersheva. The Nabateans were desert-dwelling people who had learned a secret: how to preserve sparse rainfall to irrigate crops where no one else thought they could grow.

The Nabateans greeted Honi, as it was common for them to pick up wandering people in the desert. When Honi managed to convey what he was doing, all about his carob journey, they smiled and offered to plant some of his seeds when they returned to their own settlement.

Honi and the Nabateans reached the great market of

B'ersheva. The Circlemaker felt far away from his
native Galilee; indeed it seemed as if he was in another world. Exotically dressed nomads were leading
caravans of camels and donkeys in and out of the
market, bearings all kinds of herbs and spices, dyes
and fabrics, dried fruits and olive oil. Honi stocked up
on whatever provisions he needed and bid the
Nabateans a fond farewell.

As he was leaving the market Honi heard a loud
spitting noise. A split second later he felt a peculiar
wet sensation on his neck. "Of all the nerve . . ." Honi
exclaimed as he wheeled around to identify this un-
commonly rude individual, only to be stopped in his
tracks by an irate camel baring its teeth and getting
ready to shoot another wad in Honi's direction. Honi
beat a hasty retreat as the Nabateans he had be-
friended, witnessing the incident, lay convulsed in
laughter. One of them called out to Honi, in an Ara-
maic dialect so different from his own, something to
the effect that camels should be given their space.

What happened next to Honi, however, was far from

funny. In fact, it cost the Circlemaker the rest of his journey, and very nearly cost him his life.

Honi was on his way to Gaza, intending to journey from there all along the coast of the land of Israel, past Jaffa, all the way up to Haifa, when a terrible thing happened.

The yoreh, the first rain of the new season, which generally arrives in late Tishrei or Heshvan, had begun to fall. The day was gray and cold. Honi was ambling along the road, when suddenly an armed soldier confronted him at spearpoint. As had been true during most of Honi's lifetime, what amounted to civil war was ravaging the land of Israel. Two brothers vied for the throne; in reality both were vassals of Rome. When Honi was brought to the commanding officer, the general recognized the Circlemaker.

Honi was closely interrogated by the soldiers, who were convinced he was a spy. They did not believe the Circlemaker when he told them about his journey of the last few months. Then the general said: "I have heard of all you have done and how your prayers unlock the gates of heaven. Pray for us, Circlemaker. Pray to God that we may defeat the pretender. Then we shall know that our prayers will be answered."

Honi resisted. This he could not do. It was an affront to the Almighty.

"Pray," threatened the soldiers, "or we shall know you are a spy." One of the soldiers brought his spear to Honi's neck.

Honi, shivering in the damp and cold, began reciting these words:

"Creator of the world!
Have mercy on both contending sides.
For on one side is a brother,
on the other side is a brother.
These are your children,
and these are your children.
Creator of the world:
Do not heed the curses of the one upon the other!"

The prayer so enraged the officer that he ordered Honi removed from the camp and executed. That might have been the end of the Circlemaker, had not that band of Nabatean traders passed by, the ones who had helped Honi when he was lost in the desert and taken him to the B'ersheva market. Seeing the hapless Honi being led away to an obviously unkind fate, they offered to relieve the soldier charged with

41

the execution of his burden. The skeptical soldier changed his expression when some choice commodities were pressed into his hand. When the soldier returned to the camp he reported that he had carried out the general's orders.

The Nabateans could see that the Circlemaker had suffered during his ordeal. They made arrangements for Honi to be taken home to his village. As he was leaving them, Honi asked how he could repay their kindness. For instead of Honi's helping some unfortunate souls, these modest and kind people had twice saved his life. "In what way can I repay your kindness," Honi asked, "for I am greatly in your debt."

"When you come upon a lost person, as we did, help them find their way. When you come across a person in danger, as we did, help them to safety. That is what you owe us, Circlemaker. And one other thing: Plant carobs, Circlemaker, plant carobs."

8

The End of the Circle

So Honi the Circlemaker was brought home to his village of Megilo. He was laid upon his bed, and many prayers for his recovery were offered. But Honi would take up his walk across the land of Israel no more. All he could manage, from time to time, was to prop himself up on his bed and look out his window. The Circlemaker slipped back and forth between wakefulness and sleep. When people whom he had known all his life entered the room, he did not recognize them. Honi seemed to be in a different time and place. He spoke of things that nobody could understand.

Honi himself was as perplexed as anyone around him. He was still trying to remember what had happened. He had woken up to find himself back in his village, but nothing was the same. He went walking through his village and saw a man picking the fruit of a carob tree. Honi could not understand. With his very eyes Honi had seen this carob tree planted. That had been some years ago, but nowhere near the seventy years it took for a carob tree to reach maturity. And here was the same man, or so it seemed, picking the fruit!

"Are you the man who planted the tree?" Honi asked. "Of course not," replied the man, "that was my grandfather."

Honi went to the market. No one recognized him. He inquired about a man named Honi the Circlemaker.

"The Circlemaker? He rests in peace."

Honi looked at these villagers and cried: "I am the Circlemaker!" but they only smiled politely and kept their children away from him.

Honi then went to the academy. The scholars were in the midst of a scholarly debate. "If only the Circlemaker were here to give us the answer," one of them lamented.

"I am here. I am Honi the Circlemaker." Honi was greatly pained, for the scholars only chuckled and then grew annoyed at his presence. In sorrow Honi left, repeating these words: "A man who does not enjoy the company of his fellows is as if he were dead."

Honi was still repeating those words when the people maintaining a vigil by his bedside saw the Circlemaker pull himself upright. For a moment his gaze cleared and his eyes brightened, like sun breaking through the clouds after a rainy day.

"Was I dreaming?" whispered Honi.

"We are all dreamers, dear Circlemaker."

Honi asked them: "Is it possible for a person to sleep seventy years and have the same dream?"

"Anything is possible."

"Did I walk the land of Israel?"

"None made a greater circle."

"But alas it is unfinished."

"We shall finish it, Honi the Circlemaker. We shall close the circle. We and our children and our children's children."

Whereupon Honi smiled and asked that he be brought under a particular carob tree in the village. There he gathered young and old round about. He began to chant a psalm:

Shir Hama'alot, A song of ascents:
When the Lord restores Zion,
we shall be as dreamers.
Our mouths shall be filled with laughter,
our tongues with songs of joy.

The folk joined in:

They who sow in tears
shall reap with songs of joy.

Honi continued:

The one who goes along weeping,
carrying the seed-bag,
shall return with songs of joy

The people answered:

Carrying his sheaves
shall return with songs of joy.

And the Circlemaker came to the end of the circle,
which is also the beginning.

Barry L. Schwartz, rabbi at Temple Sinai in Amherst, New York, has a wide background in Jewish ecological and historical concerns. In addition to his work on folktales, he is a founding member of *Shomrei Adamah* (a Jewish environmental organization) and is completing a book on Judaism and ecology. Rabbi Schwartz was ordained in 1985 at the Hebrew Union College in New York, and served Congregation Ohel Avraham in Haifa, Israel for three years. He is also author of the high school text, *Jewish Theology: A Comparative Study.*